NOAH

POINTING TO JESUS (BOOK 1)

MAX & JASON STRANGE

Drawings by
MAX STRANGE

Colored by
MIKE RUOLNGUL

Twinhouse
Publishing

FREE STARTER LIBRARY

Get Max & Jason Strange's Starter Library for Free

Sign-up for our no-spam newsletter filled with funny stories from our childhood, along with 2 inspiring Children's ebook pdf's, children's coloring book, and much more exclusive content — all for free.

- No-Spam Newsletter
- Funny "Strange Tales" Personal Stories
- The Scared Pirate Boy ebook (pdf)
- Andy's BIG Antlers ebook (pdf)
- Childrens Coloring Book
- Other Cool Freebies and Artwork

Go here to get Jason & Max's starter Library

=> https://twinhousepublishing.com/books

Printed in the United States of America
Noah: Pointing to Jesus
First Printing, © 2018

Twinhouse Publishing
28 Montgomery Ln
Springboro, Oh 45066

https://twinhousepublishing.com/books

Ordering Information:
Quantity sales. Special discounts are available on quantity purchases by corporations, associations, and others.
For details, contact the publisher at the address above.

Pointing to Jesus Series is dedicated to our kids.
Noah-Selah-Seanna-Aurelius-Eden.
Elliana-Avalyn-Haddon

To Christian parents who pray that their children treasure Jesus above all
else. To kids everywhere who are ready for the greatest adventure of all...
which is found not in a Place or a Thing, but in a Person!
He is none other than JESUS, the Lord of Glory.

TABLE OF CONTENTS

I'd rather see Jesus where He isn't, than to miss Him where He is."

— CHARLES HADDON SPURGEON

Then Jesus said to them, "You foolish people! You find it so hard to believe all that the prophets wrote in the Scriptures. Wasn't it clearly predicted that the Messiah would have to suffer all these things before entering his glory?" Then Jesus took them through *the writings of Moses* and *all the prophets,* explaining from all the Scriptures the things concerning himself."

— LUKE 24:25-27

Dear Parents,

On that famous Road to Emmaus, two disciples encountered the resurrected Lord Jesus. In that story, Jesus gave them a new way to read their Old Testament.

Luke records,

> **And beginning with Moses and all the Prophets, he interpreted to them in all the Scriptures the things concerning himself."**
>
> — LUKE 24:27 ESV

In a sense, Jesus hands them a *"lens,"* a *"pair of glasses,"* or a new *"framework."* He opened their hearts to understand how the whole Old Testament points to Himself.

What was the result? They said, "Did not our hearts burn within us while he talked to us on the road, while he opened to us the Scriptures."

We've taken **the Emmaus Road** idea in our approach to writing this series. It is our prayer that children, in all the churches and in all the world, will experience that flame within the heart, that heart-burn, as they understand the Old Testament in light of Jesus.

Parents will also notice that there are whole Bible connections to the short stories as you read. What we mean is that **the whole Bible is used to interpret the story.** We are using Scripture to interpret

Scripture. We made sure that God's Word in total, as best as we humanly and prayerfully could, bears upon each narrative.

Our desire was to have a *canonical* (whole Bible) richness to the immediate story without detracting from the flow of the story. We did this because we feel that this is the natural way that Christians now read the Word of God.

Being on this side of the Cross, we consciously engage the Story with the Spirit of Christ and are in some way compelled to see how the stories are moving with Christ-centered clues and queues.

The Spirit Himself has so inspired the Word of God since its inception, so that we would experience God's Word in this way.

It was our hope to highlight the shadows, the types, the promises and fulfillments, that point to Jesus.

In addition, we did our best to stay away from artwork that would portray the Bible as mythical or as if were an unreal comic book adventure.

We wanted the characters to be real and the scenes to feel realistic so that your children would know that these people, places and events did in fact really happen in time and space.

Lastly, we are also trying to provide fun, short, readable, engaging stories for kids that do more than simply point to some moral example or some pattern for behavior.

The Old Testament is far more God-glorifying, Christ-exalting, and

Spirit-illuminating when we too wear those same glasses given on the Emmaus Road. Those glasses were Jesus Himself.

Simply put, it is our great endeavor that these brief stories point your children to Jesus.

Lastly, we firmly believe ALL Scripture is breathed out by God (2 Tim. 3:16; 2 Peter 1:20-21), and that there is nothing in scripture that is incidental or random.

God, by His Spirit is always communicating truths that have an impact on the immediate story and the bigger picture as well. To us, this highlights Gods supremacy over all history, and specifically Gods Redemptive Storyline. He is the Author.

✪ This star is there to help you make those connections. There are many connections, but due to the short nature of this book we could only list a few.

~ Max & Jason Strange

~

GENESIS 6-9

You clothed the earth with floods of water,
water that covered even the mountains.
At your command, the water fled;
at the sound of your thunder, it hurried away.
Mountains rose and valleys sank
to the levels you decreed.
Then you set a firm boundary for the seas,
so they would never again cover the earth.
Psalm 104:6-9

~

"Christ is the visible image of the invisible God.
He existed before anything was created
and is supreme over all creation,
for through him God created everything in the heavenly realms and
on earth.
He made the things we can see
and the things we can't see—
such as thrones, kingdoms, rulers, and authorities
in the unseen world.
Everything was created through him and for him.
He existed before anything else,
and he holds all creation together."
— Colossians 1:15-17 NLT

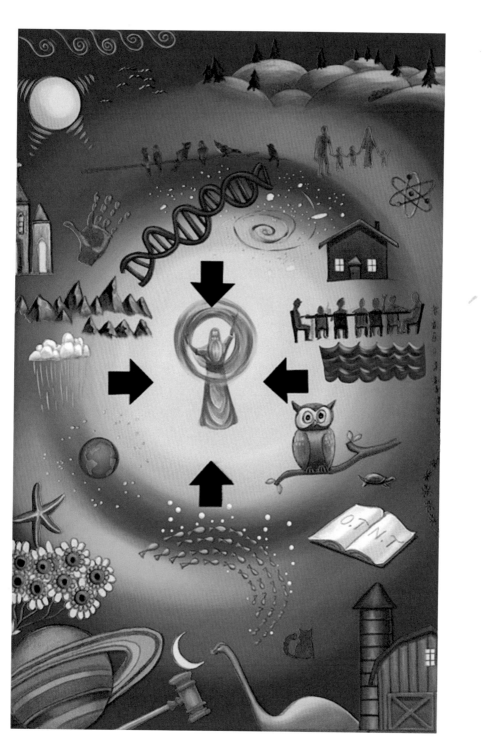

A long, long, time ago, the world was in **BIG, BIG trouble.** It was full of people who did not love God. Everything they thought and did saddened God.

Sin had flooded the hearts of all mankind, and so sin had flooded the whole world attaching itself to everything.

This made the world a very dark and scary place to live.

God didn't want that kind of world any longer. So, God planned to unmake the world.... A new world was coming.

NOAH

66 The Lord observed the extent of human wickedness on
the earth, and he saw that everything they thought or
imagined was consistently and totally evil. So the Lord
was sorry he had ever made them and put them on the
earth. **IT BROKE HIS HEART.** And the Lord said, "I
will wipe this human race I have created from the face
of the earth. Yes, and I will destroy every living thing—
all the people, the large animals, the small animals that
scurry along the ground, and even the birds of the sky. I
am sorry I ever made them."

— GENESIS 6:5-6

A nd because of this the people on earth had forgotten about
the true and living God.

Everyone did whatever they wanted, and they did not care about
God. They thought they could live without God.

When sin controls the heart, it blinds each person from the truth of
God and locks them into spiritual darkness.

n turning from God, people create fake gods to worship. They worshiped things they made: animals, trees, other people, insects, he Sun, the moon, and the stars. You name it, they worshiped it!

They worshiped everything BUT God! So, God planned to wash the vorld of all this evil and start over.

The whole creation was about to become..."UNMADE."

B ut first, in order to point to Jesus, God would appoint a man named Noah. Noah believed in God and this is his story...

66 Noah was a righteous man, the only blameless person living on earth at the time, and he walked in close fellowship with God.

— GENESIS 6:9B

God planned to make Noah "a savior" for all who would also believe in God.

✪ Just as Noah was soon to save "his house," in the future Jesus would one day become 'The Savior' to all those in His house. Jesus too would come to save his family, the Church. The chosen people of God.

~

G od told Noah,

66 So God said to Noah, "I have decided to destroy all living creatures, for they have filled the earth with violence. Yes, I will wipe them all out along with the earth!"

— GENESIS 6:12-13

God's plan was to restart the whole earth by covering it with water. God would wash away the people and their sins. In its place, God would create a new world, a new creation.

So, if the whole world was to drown in this world-wide flood, how would Noah, his family, and many animals be saved?

~

G od spoke to Noah and told him to build an Ark by His measurements.

You might ask, "What is an ark?"

An ark is a gigantic boat made to PROTECT and keep SAFE all who would be INSIDE. Noah and his family needed this safety because God's anger on sin was coming soon!

God told Noah exactly how to build this huge Ark. This boat would have a roof, a window, and three floors. It would be able to hold every kind of animal that was in the world at that time.

> Build a large boat from cypress wood and waterproof it with tar, inside and out. Then construct decks and stalls throughout its interior. Make the boat 450 feet long, 75 feet wide, and 45 feet high."

— GENESIS 6:14-15

For over one year, the ark would be a place where God would be with Noah and his family.

○ One day, Jesus would become an Ark for His people.

He would come and tell everyone that He was the only way to find PROTECTION, SAFETY, PEACE, and FORGIVENESS. Everyone in Jesus would be safe from God's judgment!

'I have told you all this so that you may have peace in me. Here on earth you will have many trials and sorrows. But take heart, because I have overcome the world." ~ John 16:33

~

So, like Jesus, Noah too was a great preacher who was righteous, blameless and walked with God. ✪

Noah, may have used the ark to call out to the people.

REPENT! COME INSIDE THE ARK! BE SAVED! BE SAVED FROM THE JUDGMENT TO COME!"

Sadly, no one believed Noah's message except for Noah's family. Only eight in all the world would be saved.

> ...he (God) did not spare the ancient world, but preserved Noah, a herald (preacher) of righteousness..."
>
> — 2 PETER 2:5

> The Lord isn't really being slow about his promise, as some people think. No, he is being patient for your sake. He does not want anyone to be destroyed, but wants everyone to repent."
>
> — 2 PETER 3:9

A fter 100 years, Noah had finished what God called him to do. The hard work of building the ark and of preaching was finished.

❂ **In the future, Jesus would come and likewise, finish all the work needed to save His people.**

" I glorified you on earth, having accomplished the work that you gave me to do." ~Jesus

— JOHN 17:4

" So Noah did everything exactly as God had commanded him."

— GENESIS 6:22

Now it was time to fill the Ark.

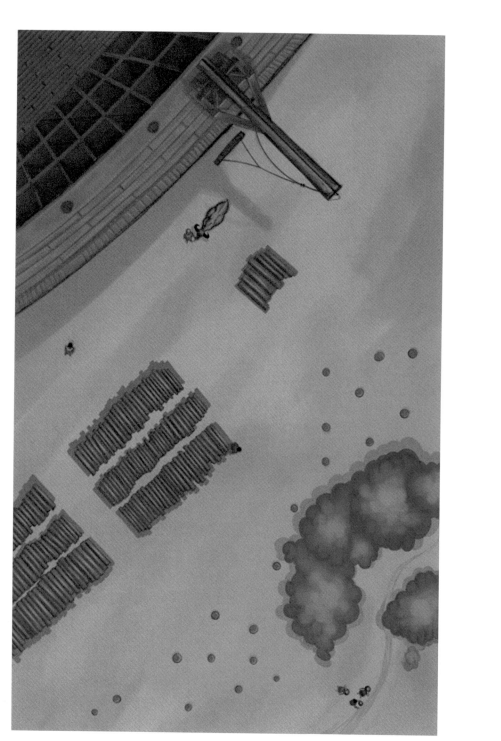

G od caused creatures from all over the earth to begin their march towards the ark.

The creatures marched from the forest
and from the jungles.
They walked down from the highlands
and up from the lowlands.
They strolled across plains
and trotted over the mountains.
Most came by two and some came by seven.
Some flew in and some crawled in.
Some hopped in and some slithered in.
Some ran in and some stomped in.

Even though sin had made a big mess of the world, God wanted to save the animals of the earth. He made sure that his creatures would also have a future alongside man.

When everything was ready, the Lord said to Noah, "Go into the boat with all your family, for among all the people of the earth, I can see that you alone are righteous. Take with you seven pairs—male and female —of each animal I have approved for eating and for sacrifice, and take one pair of each of the others. Also take seven pairs of every kind of bird. There must be a male and a female in each pair to ensure that all life will survive on the earth after the flood. Seven days from now I will make the rains pour down on the earth. **And it will rain for forty days and forty nights**, until I have wiped from the earth all the living things I have created."

— Genesis 7:1-4

~

Now, this Ark was designed with only one door. There was no other way to get in or get out! This door was the only way of salvation. The only way to avoid Gods wrath.

To get to the new world that God was going to make, every creature would have to go through that ONE DOOR.

✪ One day Jesus would become THE DOOR of salvation and say,

> So Jesus again said to them, "Truly, truly, I say to you, **I am the door of the sheep.** All who came before me are thieves and robbers, but the sheep did not listen to them. **I am the door.** If anyone enters by me, he will be saved and will go in and out and find pasture." ~ John 10:7-9

God closed the door behind them. Only those who were shut in the ark would be safe. Nothing could get in and nothing could go out.

✪ A wooden boat would become their salvation, just as a wooden CROSS would one day become the salvation of God's people.

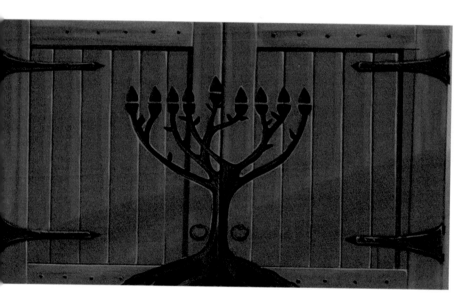

~

Jesus told the story of another door that would one day be shut. It had to do with a big wedding feast and how bridesmaids were waiting for the bridegroom to come.

Half of the bridesmaids were ready and half were not. When the bridegroom finally came, the ones who were ready made it in. The others were not ready and the door was shut.

> And while they were going to buy, the bridegroom came, and those who were ready went in with him to the marriage feast, and the door was shut."

— MATTHEW 25:10

Inside the ark now, Noah gathered his family and prayed for God's protection and that all would safely make it through the Storm of God's anger.

Noah lifted his arms, prayed with wife, his three sons, Ham, Shem, Japheth and their wives.

He continued to trust God in an obeying way.

~

The earth shook terribly and the great fountains of the deep within the earth burst open. Deep waters under the earth exploded outwards. ~ Genesis 7:11

The windows of heaven opened up too, and poured down rain. Water poured down from above and came up from below.

It rained, and rained, and then it rained some more. It rained for 40 days and 40 nights.

The waters increased greatly and lifted the ark higher and higher above the earth towards the sky.

The waters filled up every hill and valley.

Noah and his family were lifted above the judgments beneath them and kept safe by God.

I n all the destruction, God was with Noah and his family.

My people will abide in a peaceful habitation, in secure dwellings, and in quiet resting places."

— ISAIAH 32:18

This was to fulfill the word that he had spoken: Of those whom you gave me I have lost not one."

— JOHN 18:9

~

Even the highest mountains on earth were covered by the world-wide flood.

Every animal that moved on the earth, birds, livestock, beasts, and yucky bugs all died.

> God wiped out every living thing on the earth—people, livestock, small animals that scurry along the ground, and the birds of the sky. All were destroyed. The only people who survived were Noah and those with him in the boat."

— GENESIS 7:23

~

Sadly, out of all the people on the earth, only Noah and his family were alive.

✪ However one day, from Noah's family, the greatest thing would happen! Someone from the family line of Noah would one day be born. He would be the true Savior of the world...The Lord and only Savior, Jesus Christ!

If Noah wouldn't have been saved, then there would have been no Jesus.

No Noah, No Jesus!
No Jesus, No Way of Salvation
No Salvation, No Hope

Good thing we have a Wonderful God who is:

- Patient
- Kind
- Holy
- Loving
- Full of Grace

NOAH

~

" But God remembered Noah and all the wild animals and livestock with him in the boat. He sent a wind to blow across the earth, and the floodwaters began to recede (go down). The underground waters stopped flowing, and the torrential rains from the sky were stopped. So the floodwaters gradually receded from the earth. After 150 days, exactly five months from the time the flood began, the boat came to rest on the mountains of Ararat. Two and a half months later, as the waters continued to go down, other mountain peaks became visible."

— Genesis 8:1-5

Slowly the earth drained and day after day Noah and his family trusted God as they waited.

Finally, the Ark hit something! It got stuck and RESTED on a mountain called Ararat.

NOAH

~

Noah first released a raven that flew out from the ark. Every time it would fly back because it had nowhere to land.

Noah then released a dove and after several trips it came back with an olive branch. This meant the water was going down and dry land was beginning to appear.

He then released the dove one more time, and this time it never came back. This was the sign. It was almost time to get off the ark!

- Can you imagine the excitement of Noah and his family?
- Can you imagine being the only people on Earth?

" Then God said to Noah, "Leave the boat, all of you— you and your wife, and your sons and their wives. Release all the animals—the birds, the livestock, and the small animals that scurry along the ground—so they can be fruitful and multiply throughout the earth."
~ Genesis 8:15-17

The Dove Fly's Back to Noah's hand

T he Day had come! Noah and his family stepped into a remade world, a new creation.

✪ One day, Jesus will come back. Everyone who is "In Jesus," is already apart of the New Creation that Jesus started.

❝ Therefore, if anyone is in Christ, he is **a new creation**. The old has passed away; behold, the new has come."

— 2 CORINTHIANS 5:17

- Jesus is the ONLY Safe Place
- Jesus is the ONLY Ark
- Jesus is the ONLY Door

❝ But we are looking forward to the **new heavens** and **new earth** he has promised, a world filled with God's righteousness.

— 2 PETER 3:13

N oah thanked God for His love and faithfulness.

He built an altar and worshiped God with a sacrifice because not all things were made new. Sin was still tucked inside the heart.

> And the Lord was pleased with the aroma of the sacrifice and said to himself, "I will never again curse the ground because of the human race, even though everything they think or imagine is bent toward evil from childhood. **I will never again destroy all living things.** As long as the earth remains, there will be planting and harvest, cold and heat, summer and winter, day and night."
>
> — GENESIS 8:21-22

✪ God's plan all along was not to just wash away sins with water, but to wash away our sins forever through a **Perfect Sacrifice**. Jesus' sacrifice would destroy sin forever. This aroma would please God for all time.

~

God's Judgment did come again, but it didn't come upon the world with water. It came upon Jesus, God's one and only Son. ✪

On the cross he was drowned with the sins of the world. He was punished for you, for me.

> For Christ also suffered once for sins, the righteous for the unrighteous, that he might bring us to God, being put to death in the flesh but made alive in the spirit, in which he went and proclaimed to the spirits in prison, because they formerly did not obey, **when God's patience waited in the days of Noah, while the ark was being prepared, in which a few, that is, eight persons, were brought safely through water.**"
>
> — I PETER 3:18-20

✪ Jesus did this to take my sins from me. This is why we need Jesus so badly. This is why we need a Savior. God has made the Way for us to be forgiven...forever.

~

G od placed His glory in the sky, called a bow (rainbow) to show that He would never flood the world again.

> Then God said, "I am giving you **a sign of my covenant (promise)** with you and with all living creatures, for all generations to come. I have placed **my rainbow** in the clouds. It is the sign of my covenant with you and with all the earth. When I send clouds over the earth, the rainbow will appear in the clouds, and I will remember my covenant with you and with all living creatures." —

It was a beautiful colorful sign in the sky. **An unbreakable promise** for all time.

In the future Gods peace would be displayed in a cross, not the

❝ When the Son of Man returns, **it will be like it was** *in Noah's day*. In those days before the flood, the people were enjoying banquets and parties and weddings right up to the time Noah entered his boat. People didn't realize what was going to happen until the flood came and swept them all away. That is the way it will be when the Son of Man comes. "Two men will be working together in the field; one will be taken, the other left. Two women will be grinding flour at the mill; one will be taken, the other left. *"So you, too, must keep watch!* For you don't know what day your Lord is coming."

— MATTHEW 24: 37-42

❝ By faith Noah, **being warned by God concerning events as yet unseen, in reverent fear constructed an ark for the saving of his household.** By this he condemned the world and became an heir of the righteousness that comes by faith."

— HEBREWS 11:7

Most importantly, I want to remind you that in the last days scoffers will come, mocking the truth and following their own desires. They will say, "What happened to the promise that **Jesus is coming again?** From before the times of our ancestors, everything has remained the same since the world was first created."

They deliberately forget that **God made the heavens long ago by the word of his command,** and he brought the earth out from the water and surrounded it with water. **Then he used the water to destroy the ancient world with a mighty flood.**

The Lord isn't really being slow about his promise, as some people think. No, he is being patient for your sake. **He does not want anyone to be destroyed, but wants everyone to repent.** But the day of the Lord will come as unexpectedly as a thief." ~ 2 Peter 3:3-6,9-10

Notice the 3 Things that the world forgets:

1. Jesus is coming again
2. God made the heavens long ago by his word
3. The Mighty Flood during Noah's time

ABOUT THE AUTHOR'S

MAX & JASON STRANGE

Max strange is an emerging author of the 'Pointing to Jesus series' along with several upcoming new releases including, "Hones Princess Normaline" Trilogy. Not too long ago he teamed up with his twin brother to form Twinhouse Publishing.

Jason Strange is the author of the upcoming series, "The Tree & the Light," Trilogy, and "Everlite: The Quilted Princess." He has multiple children books that are on the way, and often has too many ideas (a good thing). To date, he has over 25 (maybe more) books stewing in his creative crock pot.

Facebook: http://bit.ly/FBTwinhousePub

Twitter: twitter.com/JasonRStrange

COMING SOON

Coming Soon: 20 Book Series, "Pointing to Jesus"

1. Pointing to Jesus: Jonah
2. Pointing to Jesus: Samson
3. Pointing to Jesus: King Nebuchadnezzar
4. Pointing to Jesus: Joseph

By Jason:

1. Everlite: The Quilted Princess 2018
2. The Super Dupers 2018
3. A Field Trip to the Stratus 2018

By Max:

1. Honest Princess Normaline Trilogy 2018-2019
2. The Webster Saga 2018

Made in the USA
Lexington, KY
11 April 2018